Rainforests

First published in 2015 by
Franklin Watts,
338 Euston Road,
London NW1 3BH

Created and produced by:
Green Android Ltd,
49 Beaumont Court, Upper Clapton Road,
London E5 8BG, United Kingdom
www.greenandroid.co.uk

ISBN 978-1-4451-3742-1
Dewey number: 333.75

Franklin Watts is a division of Hachette Children's Books,
An Hachette UK company
www.hachette.co.uk

Photo credits:
Images © www.flpa-images.co.uk: harpy eagle (7), green anaconda (15) © Pete Oxford/Minden Pictures/FLPA; flying lemur (7) © Suzi Eszterhas/Minden Pictures/FLPA. Images © Shuutterstock.com: floating village (26) © abonjoch; amazon rainforest (5) © achiaos; blue dyeing dart frog, strawberry poison dart frog (23) © Aleksey Stemmer; giant owl butterfly (5) © Ammit Jack; jaguar (cov) © amskad; huli (27), huli tribe (cov) © Amy Nichole Harris; jaguar (17) © Anan Kaewkhammul; durian (24) © Andrey Tarantin; harlequin poison dart frog (23) © Anneka; howler monkey (8) © Anton_Ivanov; stick insect (11) © Antonio Clemens; ganoderma (29) © apiguide; winged seeds (7) © Arun Roisri; woman with bananas (28) © Carlos Neto; panther chameleon (23) © Cathy Keifer; Black bear (5) © Critterbiz; lianas (9) © Daimond Shutter; little-Bee Eater (19) © Dave Montreuil; bark (9) © Denis Filatov; toco Toucan (19) © Dennis Jacobsen; fog tropical forest (1) © dioch; daintree flower (4) © Dirk Ercken; rainforest (2), giant tree (4), kapok tree (7), rainforest, treefrog eggs (10), ants (11), slime mould (13), wasp nest, Leaf-cutter ants, bush cricket, wandering spider (21), cocoa pods (27) © Dr. Morley Read; bushbaby (17) © EcoPrint; squirrel monkey (32) © Eduardo Rivero; prayer plant (11) © EllenSmile; hot lips (11) © Elliotte Rusty Harold; agouti (13), tapir (13), Margay (17) © Erni; madagascar gecko (22) © Fedor Selivanov; kamayurá fisherman (27) © Frontpage; oriental whipsnake (23) © gopause; rainforest destroyed by fire (31) © guentermanaus; tropical rainforest tree (cov) © Gwoeii; blue morpho (7) © hagit berkovich; piranha (15) © Hayati Kayhan; poinsettia (25) © Heather Snow; hoatzin (19) © hecke61; dani (27), orangutan (31) © javarman; bearded pig (17) © Julian W; lori Lorikeet (19) © jurra8; treeshrew (17) © kajornyot; flying Foxes (17) © KAMONRAT; rafflesia (25) © Kiwisoul; rafflesia (cov) © kkaplin; waxy leaves (7) © KPG_Payless; water lily (14), Cocoa Pod (29) © Ksenia Ragozina; palm oil industry (29) © KYTan; coati (13), squirrel monkey (16) © l i g h t p o e t; tongass rainforest (5), temperate rainforest floor (cov) © Lee Prince; cherimoya (29) © LianeM; marmosets (9) © Luiz Antonio da Silva; karen woman (26) © M R; tree frog in canna lily (24) © Mark Bridger; temperate rainforest (5) © Matt Tilghman; drip tip (9) © Matthew Cole; jaguar (12) © Mikadun; zebra plant (11) © Nainong; sloth (17) © nattanan726; nepenthe (25) © Nengloveyou; blue morpho (cov) © Nicky Rhodes; extracting latex (29) © OlegD; macaws (18) © ostill; tropical rainforest (5) © Pablo Hidalgo - Fotos593; batwa (27) © Pal Teravagimov; pink-toed tarantula (21) © Patrick K. Campbell; epiphytes (25) © Phil Syme; hmong (27) © Pornsak Paewlumfaek; congo river (15) © Przemyslaw Skibinski; daintree rainforest (5) © Ralph Loesche; millipede (cov) © reptiles4all; rainforest being destroyed (30) © Rich Carey; capybaras (15) © Roberto Tetsuo Okamura; papaya (29) ©Roobcio; millipede (21) © Ryan M. Bolton; great Hornbill (8) © Sainam51; emergent layer (7) © Sara Berdon; hummingbird (6) © Sari ONeal; baka hunter (27) © Sergey Uryadnikov; heliconia (25) © Shulevskyy Volodymyr; tropical rainforest (cov) © sittitap; fog in rainforest (6) © Stephane Bidouze; rhinoceros beetle (21) © Stubblefield Photography; bromeliad (25) © Supavadee butradee; bananas (30) © Thinglass; amazon river (14) © thobo; tree (8) © THPStock; peace Lily (11) © topimages; rattan workers (28) © utcon; mekong river (15) © Viet Images; buttress roots (13) © Vilainecrevette; dwarf caiman (23) © Vitaly Raduntsev; orinoco river (15) © Vladimir Melnik; river turtle (22) © Vladislav T. Jirousek; mossy branches (9) © welcomia; golden orb spider (21) © Yongkiet jitwattanatam; rainforest (12) © zstock; Logging truck (31) © Lisette van der Hoorn.

Introduction

There are no environments on Earth more mysterious and complex than rainforests. These incredible forests cover just six per cent of the Earth's surface, yet are home to over half of all identified animal and plant species. Rainforests are characterised by high rainfall and fast-growing trees. They are also vital for the wellbeing of our planet. They recycle carbon dioxide into oxygen and are crucial for stabilising global climate and controlling climate change.

Contents

Read on to **find** out more about the **Earth's** rainforests...

What is a rainforest?

Rainforests are very special places with an enormous **variety** of animal and plant life. **Rainforests** are found on every **continent** on Earth, except Antarctica. There are two main types of rainforest. **Tropical** rainforests are found in the tropics, close to the **equator**, where the climate is hot all year round. **Temperate** rainforests are found further away from the tropics, often along coasts. They have hot **summers** and cold winters. Both types of **rainforests** are very wet places that get plenty of **sunlight** and warmth.

A giant rainforest tree in the Amazon rainforest

Some rainforests soak up a massive 400 centimetres of rain every year!

Largest tropical

The Amazon rainforest in South America is the largest tropical rainforest. It covers an area of over five million square kilometres.

Largest temperate

The world's largest temperate rainforests can be found on North America's Pacific coast. These rainforests stretch from northern California and into Canada.

Did you know?

The Daintree rainforest in northeast Australia is the world's oldest, intact tropical lowland rainforest. Eighty per cent of the flowers in the Daintree are found nowhere else in the world.

A tropical rainforest in Ecuador

A temperate rainforest in the USA

Factfile

Famous rainforests

Rainforests only occupy six per cent of the planet, but they play a critical part in its health. They are called 'the lungs of the world'.

Amazon rainforest
Smaller than Australia, but larger than India, this tropical rainforest runs through nine South American countries.

Daintree rainforest
This tropical Australian rainforest runs along the Daintree River to the sea. It has some of the earliest plants found on Earth.

Tropical and temperate forests

Tropical rainforests are complex environments with four levels: forest floor, understory, canopy and emergent. They are dominated by tall trees with smooth bark, often draped in vines seeking sunlight above the canopy. Most animal life is in the trees, which is where they find food.

Temperate rainforests have three levels: forest floor, understory and canopy. They are dominated by tall conifer (bearing cones and needles) trees, but there are medium and small trees as well. Ferns, mosses and small plants cover the rich soil, which is where most animal life is found.

A giant owl butterfly from a tropical rainforest

Full of life

Rainforests are home to half of all animal species in the world and scientists know there are thousands more to be discovered. Insects are the largest group of animals that live in rainforests. Animals compete for food and shelter, and many species are endangered or are already extinct.

Tongass National Forest
A temperate rainforest in southeastern Alaska, USA, it consists of islands, fjords, glaciers and vast stretches of coastline.

A black bear from a temperate rainforest

Layers of the rainforest

When scientists are studying rainforests, they divide the **forest** into layers. Though each **layer** has things in common with other layers, they each have different **temperatures**, receive varying amounts of **moisture**, contain different levels of sunlight and host a diversity of animal and plant life. The **highest** level in a tropical rainforest is the **emergent** layer. Emergent trees grow up through the other **layers**, but they are widely spaced and have umbrella-shaped tops. They spread their **foliage** out wide so their leaves catch as much **sunlight** as possible.

During the rainy season, the bird-eating tarantula spider stalks its prey in the emergent layer.

Did you know?

Over 300 species of hummingbird are found in the emergent layer of the Amazon rainforest. The wings of these beautiful birds beat so rapidly that they make a humming sound.

Tall and wide

Trees in the emergent layer can reach a height of 70 metres. The base of their trunks can grow to five metres in diameter.

Falling fruit

The Brazil nut tree is one of the tallest in the emergent layer of the Amazon. Its falling fruit, which contains the nuts, hurtles to the ground at speeds of 80 kilometres per hour!

The emergent layer visible through the fog of a rainforest in Thailand

Umbrella shaped trees
of the emergent layer

Factfile
Emergent tree adaptations

Emergent trees have developed in special ways so they can survive and take advantage of their exposed position.

Spreading out

Emergent trees spread their foliage to maximize the capture of sunlight, water and carbon dioxide for photosynthesis.

Waxy leaves

The leaves are often small and waxy. The waxy coating helps to retain moisture in drying winds and hot temperatures.

Winged seeds

Emergent trees can use the wind to carry their seeds – some of which are winged – away from the ground below the tree.

Umbrella shapes

Trees that reach up to the emergent layer are often umbrella-shaped. This allows them to make energy from photosynthesis, but also provides animals with nesting sites, lookouts to find prey and a safe perch away from predators. Gliders and fliers can also zoom in and around the branches.

Warming up

The striking blue morpho butterfly can be found in the tropical rainforests of Latin America from Mexico to Colombia. At night it hangs from branches or from the underside of leaves in the emergent layer. After resting, the butterfly will spread its wings to warm in the sunshine.

A blue morpho
warming its wings

Predator

The harpy eagle is one of the largest and most powerful birds of prey. It hunts in the canopy and emergent layers of Central and South American rainforests. It uses its inward-pointing claws to stab and squeeze prey, such as sloths, reptiles and monkeys. This vertically diving eagle weighs just nine kilogrammes.

A harpy eagle watches
and listens for prey

In the canopy

The busiest and **noisiest** part of the rainforest is the canopy layer, which is below the emergent. The **canopy** contains most of the **wildlife** and plants. All around is the sound of monkeys screeching and birds calling. This area is made up of **tangled** branches and vines. **Sunlight**, wind and rain reach the canopy, so **fruits** and flowers grow here in abundance and there is always food for animals to eat. Some animals, like **birds**, bats and insects, fly around the canopy with ease. Some, like monkeys, **squirrels** and lizards, are adept **climbers**. Others hop, leap or glide!

The **canopy** is the **primary** layer in a **rainforest**, **forming** a roof over the **lower** layers.

A great hornbill resting in the canopy layer

Did you know?

The howler monkey is known for the howls it makes at the start and end of the day. The howls are so loud they can be heard through the dense Amazon rainforest for five kilometres.

Beetle mania

Scientists found 950 different types of beetles living on just one tree in a rainforest in Panama, Central America.

Hard to reach

To study the canopy, scientists used to fell trees, shoot down branches and one even trained a monkey to get samples. Mountaineering methods are used today.

Dripping in moss

Mosses and lichens are more typical of temperate than of tropical rainforests. They grow on other plants, but do not cause the host damage as they usually make their own food. Maple trees host more mosses than any other temperate tree. Mosses thrive in the canopy's misty, damp atmosphere.

Mossy tree branches in a temperate rainforest, in USA

Common marmosets in the canopy

Monkeying around

Rainforest monkeys, such as howler, spider, capuchin, squirrel, tamarin and marmoset, all live in the canopy. They choose the canopy to avoid the predators above and below them. They have favourite routes through the canopy and these branches are usually worn free of moss.

Gliders

Gliders have adaptations, such as webbed feet and membranes between their limbs. They can drop from a branch and steer (usually by shifting their weight or moving a tail or a limb) to another branch. There are gliding snakes, frogs, lizards and lemurs.

Limb membranes on a Sunda flying lemur

Factfile
Adaptations to canopy life

Plants develop features to survive in the canopy's humidity, still air and low amounts of sunlight. Here are three examples.

Bark
The bark is thin because it doesn't need to retain moisture. It is also smooth to discourage other plants from growing on it.

Drip tips
Canopy leaves are pointed, smooth and glossy so rainwater runs off quickly. This prevents the growth of fungus and bacteria.

Lianas
These climbing vines have their roots in the ground, while the stems climb all the way up to the canopy towards the sunlight.

In the **understory**

Under the **canopy** but above the ground it is warm and damp. Plants intertwine into a tangle of **ferns**, palms, young trees, shorter trees, **shrubs** and flowering plants. Most of the plants in the understory have large leaves to maximize **absorption** of any light that reaches this layer. Plants in this level of a **rainforest** hardly ever grow **taller** than four metres. In a tropical rainforest, you would find plenty of insects along with bats, **monkeys**, lizards, **frogs**, snakes and jaguars. In a temperate rainforest understory live deer, voles, **porcupines**, hares, black bears and many more.

Bats are attracted to flowers that smell of meat and sweat.

The understory layer of an Ecuadorian rainforest

Did you know?

The red-eyed tree frog lays eggs on the underside of a leaf that is over a pond or river. When the eggs hatch, the fluid inside the eggs helps wash the tadpoles into the water below.

Armies of ants

In the tropical rainforest, ants are everywhere. Researchers have found over 200 species of ants on a single tree!

Perfect for hiding

Some larger rainforest animals, such as jaguars, spend many hours in the gloomy light of the understory. They survey the area, looking for any tasty prey to pass by.

Hot lips flower in the
Amazon rainforest

Colourful flowers

Pollination is how flowers in the understory reproduce. As there is little wind in a rainforest, plants can't rely on the wind to transfer pollen between plants. Instead they use insects, bats and birds to do the job for them. They attract these animals using strong scents and bright colours.

Hidden creatures

To avoid being eaten or to hide themselves while hunting, many rainforest creatures use camouflage. A stick insect is easily mistaken for a twig, the spots on a jaguar's coat help it blend into the shadows and a moth's colour and shape can make it look like a piece of bark.

A stick insect in a
Ecuadorian rainforest

Factfile

Understory plants

Many plants that we keep in our homes today were originally from the understory. Both places share a lack of sunlight.

Prayer plant
At night, the leaves of this Amazonian plant fold together resembling hands closed in prayer. In the morning, they rustle open.

Zebra plant
The strong white veins on its leaves resemble the stripes on a zebra's coat. It originates from the rainforests of Brazil.

Peace lily
This plant is native to the tropical rainforests of the Americas and Southeast Asia. It helps to clean the air of chemical pollutants.

Ants on the move

Ants will relocate their colony if a queen ant is in danger or if the nest is too dry or small, or if infected or damaged. Worker ants take half the brood of pupae and larvae to the new nest before moving the queen – who is protected by guard ants – and then finally, the rest of the brood is moved.

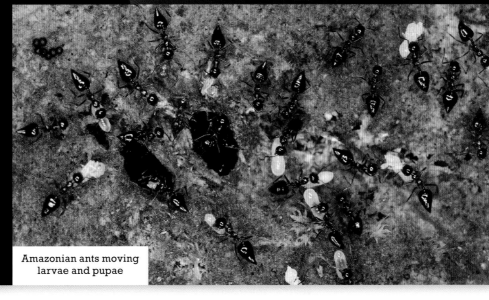

Amazonian ants moving
larvae and pupae

On the **forest floor**

The **rainforest** floor lies beneath the emergent, canopy and understory layers. Almost no **sunlight** reaches into this area. It is here that **decomposition** takes place. This is the process by which **organisms** break down dead plants and animals and recycle essential materials and **nutrients**. The dark and **moist** conditions of the forest floor mean that decomposition happens very quickly. Animals in this layer range from **insects**, amphibians and reptile species to **mammals**, such as elephants, **gorillas** and rainforest pigs.

The forest floor of an Australian rainforest

Did you know?

Jaguars live in the tropical rainforests of Central and South America. They mostly hunt on the forest floor, but will also climb into trees and pounce on their prey from above.

Plants rot quickly on the forest floor thanks to the heat and moisture.

In the dark

Just two per cent of sunlight hits the rainforest floor, so only vegetation that can grow in the dark survives. Two of these survivors are moss and fungi.

Working together

Decomposers, such as ants and termites, break down fallen trees and leaves into smaller pieces that are then digested by other organisms including fungi, worms and slugs.

Shallow roots on a
rainforest floor

Factfile

Forest floor mammals

It's dark, muddy and smothered in dying plant litter, so the perfect colour for forest floor foragers and diggers to be is brown.

Agouti

Agoutis are found in the rainforests of South America. They crack open Brazil nut shells with their sharp teeth.

Coatimundi

The coatimundi is found in the rainforests of South America. It uses its sharp claws to forage for fruit, tarantulas and reptiles.

Buttress roots

Tropical rainforests trees need different roots for different jobs. Some trees have a tangled spread of roots that access nutrients in the soil, which are held in the shallow layer near the surface. Some also have buttress roots that stretch from the ground and up the trunk for over ten metres and anchor the tree to the ground.

Slime mould

Slime moulds are important to the decomposition of organic matter in rainforests. The mould feeds on dead plant material, such as logs, flowers and fruit. It secretes a special protein that helps it digest its food.

Slime mould on the
surface of a dead branch

Recycling nutrients

Mushrooms and other fungi invade rotting organic matter and break it down into nutrients that can be reused by other plants and animals. Unlike plants, these decomposers do not contain chlorophyll (the green pigment in plant cells that converts sunlight into food) so they thrive in the dark forest.

White mushrooms growing
on elephant dung

South American Tapir

A long, flexible snout holds fruit and small branches ready for eating. Tunnel-like paths take it to food and watering holes.

13

Rainforest rivers

Rainforest **rivers** are fed by a tremendous amount of rain, which is why they are the largest rivers in the world. **Hundreds**, even thousands, of tributaries and **creeks** bring rainwater into **mega-rivers** like the Amazon, Congo, Orinoco and Mekong. These rivers are **slow-moving** and brown in colour, due to the sediment that is **washed** off the land and into the water. Where **deforestation** has occurred, greater quantities of the soil are washed away making the water a **darker** brown. There are reptiles, **fish**, birds, insects and mammals in and around these rivers.

Did you know?

Giant lily pads grow in shallow waters of the Amazon River. Their leaves can measure 2.5 metres across and the flowers, 30 centimetres. A web of air-filled veins keep them afloat.

The mighty Amazon River flowing through Brazil, South America

Rainforest rivers are almost as rich in animal life as the forests themselves.

Deepest river

Central Africa's Congo River is the world's deepest river, with depths of over 220 metres. It runs through the Congo rainforest, which is the second largest rainforest in the world.

River monster

The arapaima is the largest freshwater fish, growing to three metres and 200 kilogrammes. It is found in the Amazon River.

Capybaras on the riverbank of the Amazon

Factfile

Rainforest rivers

Other than their staggering length and volume, these rivers mostly twist and turn their way across relatively flat landscapes.

Congo River

While much of the river meanders peacefully through the rainforest, it has stretches of rapids and awe-inspiring waterfalls.

Mekong River

An important trading route and fishery, it flows through six Southeast Asian countries and is 4,350 kilometres long.

River rodents

Capybaras are the largest of all rodents. They live near lakes, rivers and streams in South America. They have webbed toes, which makes them strong swimmers. They often hide in water by holding just their nose above the surface while submerging the rest of the body.

Fearsome fish

Red-bellied piranhas are found in rivers throughout South America. They prefer to scavenge on dead meat rather than hunt and kill, so stories of their predatory behaviour are exaggerated. Even so, a shoal of these razor-toothed fish can devour a whole cow quite quickly.

A shoal of red-bellied piranhas

Orinoco River

The Orinoco flows for around 2,740 kilometres and is home to a six-metre crocodile – the largest predator in South America.

Swimmer snake

Growing to over eight metres and with an enormous girth, the green anaconda is the world's largest snake. It lives in the slow-moving Amazon and Orinoco rivers. Awkward on land, it is sleek in the water. Its eyes and nostrils are on the top of its head, so it can see and breathe while the body is submerged.

A green anaconda on the riverbank

Rainforest mammals

Many species of **mammals** make their home in the hot, moist **vegetation** or in the cool rivers of the rainforest. These animals range from tiny **shrews** and wild pigs to enormous **rhinoceros** and elephants. Primates, a group of mammals that includes monkeys, apes, tarsiers and **lemurs**, are some of the most **intelligent** animals on Earth and they live almost exclusively in rainforests. Some rainforest mammals are **timid**, small and **inconspicuous**. Other rainforest mammals, such as tigers and pumas, are **fearsome** predators.

Facts and figures

On the edge
There are six rainforest mammals, including the lemur and spectacled bear, that could become extinct in 10–15 years.

Monkey business
Capuchin monkys have a special relationship with flowering trees. As the monkey laps the nectar in the flower, pollen sticks to its face. The pollen is then transferred to the next flower that the monkey feeds on.

Diversity
A ten square kilometre area of rainforest is home to 150 different species of mammals.

Lazy mammal
A sloth will barely move for up to 18 hours a day!

Special adaptation
The pink dolphin, which lives in muddy water in the Amazon River, has a flexible neck that allows it to turn its head to navigate flooded forest plains.

Blood suckers

The Amazon rainforest is the only place in the world where all three species of blood-drinking bats can be found.

Forest elephants

Rainforest elephants are smaller than other African elephants, which enables them to move through the dense forests. Their tusks are straight so they do not get caught in vegetation.

Squirrel monkeys live mostly in the canopy to avoid the larger predators below.

Did you know?

The common tree shrew inhabits the tropical forests of Southeast Asia. During the breeding season, it builds two nests: one for its young and another for itself and its mate.

A squirrel monkey's good eyesight lets it find fruit in dark, dense vegetation

Lone feline

The jaguar is a solitary animal who lives and hunts alone, except during the mating season. They hunt mostly on the ground, but will climb trees to pounce on their prey. Their jaws are strong enough to bite straight through bone. In Native American, its name means 'he who kills with one leap'.

A jaguar hunting on the forest floor

Flying foxes (fruit bats) in a tree

A two-toed sloth is built for a treetop life

Hanging around

Bats are the most abundant of all rainforest mammals. Colonies of the largest bat, the flying fox, can often be seen hanging from branches. Each bat's place in the tree is determined by its status in the colony. The most powerful males occupy the highest, safest areas, while the weaker bats occupy lower, exposed branches.

Upside down

A sloth spends most of its life hanging upside down. Its fur grows in the opposite direction to most mammals so that rain runs off its inverted body. Often totally still for long periods, the damp conditions allow algae to grow, giving its fur a green tinge.

Factfile

Nocturnal mammals

Many mammals are active during the night when temperatures are cooler, food is abundant and they are safer from predation.

Bearded pig
This long-legged pig from Southeast Asia jumps and climbs to reach fruit dislodged by gibbons. It is also a very good swimmer.

Bush baby
Large eyes, rotating ears and a loud, baby-like cry means it can hunt at night and be located by the troop in the dense canopy.

Margay
This spotted cat lives in the canopy. It is an agile and acrobatic climber and can run head-first down a tree, just like a squirrel!

Rainforest birds

More types of birds live in the **rainforests** than anywhere else on Earth. Thousands of birds **screech** and flap around the **canopy**. Rainforests are home to thousands of species of birds, including **parrots**, hornbills and toucans, and raptors like eagles, hawks and **vultures**. Some birds arrive in rainforests during the winter and return to **cooler** regions during the spring and **summer**. Brilliant colouring and loud calls and songs help these rainforest birds locate each other and **compete** for a mate in the almost **impenetrable** canopy.

Facts and figures

Hungry hummingbird
A hummingbird has to consume half its body weight in food – mostly nectar – each day.

Cassowary worry
Only 2,000 cassowaries are left in the Daintree rainforest.

Birds of paradise
With colourful plumage and head plumes, these are the most beautiful birds in the rainforests of New Guinea and Australia.

Small wingspan
The harpy eagle has a small wingspan so that it can fly through the dense canopy.

Hanging nest
The oropendola bird of Southern and Central America often weaves its basket-like nest near wasp nests. The wasps are thought to deter snakes.

Bird numbers
There are 1,500 bird species in the Amazon.

Did you know?

Macaws gather in groups (companies) on the clay cliffs of the Amazon. They eat the clay because it contains minerals that help them process the toxins found in the seeds they eat.

Macaws in danger

Of the 18 species of Amazon macaws, several are endangered, perhaps extinct. They are losing their homes due to deforestation and they are trapped for sale as exotic pets.

Canopy dwellers

Out of the four layers of a tropical rainforest, most birds live in the canopy, which is where they find food and nesting sites.

A pair of rainbow lorikeets in the Gondwana rainforests of Australia

A toco toucan in the Amazon rainforest

Colourful bill

The bright orange bill of the toco toucan can be 23 centimetres long, about the same length as its body. The bill is quite light as it is mostly hollow. It uses its beak to pluck and peel fruit. The beak also houses a long, flat tongue that helps the toucan catch insects, reptiles and nesting birds.

Stink bird

Unlike most birds, the hoatzin is a folivore – it eats leaves! Because of its diet, it produces bacteria to help digest the leaves. This causes a fermentation process that gives off the very unpleasant odour of manure. This smell has earned this unusual and clumsy bird its nickname – stink bird.

Two hoatzins in the Amazon rainforest

A toucan sleeps with its bill tucked under a wing.

Birds in abundance

A typical ten kilometre square patch of rainforest contains as many as 400 species of birds.

Parrot power

Over 300 parrot species live in rainforests. Their beak is not just for crushing food, but also acts as a 'hand' to help them climb trees.

Dangerous diet

The little bee-eater is a beautiful and colourful small bird that frequently visits the rainforests of Africa. It feeds on flying insects especially bees, wasps and hornets. It catches its prey in flight. To remove the dangerous sting from the insect, this bird repeatedly hits the insect on a hard surface.

A little bee-eater on a branch

Minibeasts

Most of the animals of the rainforest are **invertebrates**. An invertebrate has no **backbone**, and this enormous class of animals includes **insects** (such as ants, butterflies and beetles), **arachnids** (such as spiders, centipedes and scorpions), snails and worms. It is estimated there are **2.5 million** species of insects in the **rainforest**. They range from large, like the rhinoceros **beetle**, to almost invisible. The invertebrates are dominant because of their sheer **number**, diversity, reproduction rates and ability to occupy all layers of a **rainforest**.

Facts and figures

Strong ant
A leaf-cutter ant climbs 30-metre trees and carries 50 times its body weight to the nest.

Cockroaches
Most of the world's 4,000 species of cockroaches, including one the size of a hand, are found in rainforests.

Bird-eating spider
Its fangs are 2.5 centimetres long, but it also releases irritating hairs on its body to put off predators.

Fishing spider
It can weave a web underwater, but mostly catches insects and small fish by ambush.

Transparent wings
Parts of the glasswing butterfly's wings have no colour, so look like clear glass.

Killer bees
Swarms spread through the Amazon and beyond and have killed 1,000 people to date.

Don't look up!

Insects are not just found underfoot, scuttling secretly beneath moss and logs. In the rainforest they are just as likely to be in the trees among air plants (see p. 25).

Don't breathe

Blood-sucking leeches thrive in tropical rainforests. They are attracted by movement, temperature and exhalation of carbon dioxide.

Leaf-cutter ants carrying leaf pieces in the Amazon rainforest

Four square kilometres of rainforest often houses over 50,000 species of insects.

Did you know?

Paper wasps gather fibres from dead wood, which they glue together with saliva to make their umbrella-shaped, water-resistant nests. Another secretion keeps ants away.

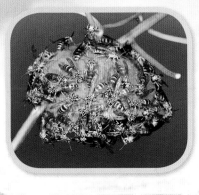

Camouflage

The rainforest bush cricket grows to a length of nine centimetres and its wings resemble leaves, giving it excellent camouflage. It has long rear legs for jumping and the male makes a buzzing sound to attract a mate.

Many legs

The giant fire millipede is found in the rainforests of Madagascar. Its body is a striking black and blood red colour, with bright red or golden legs. It grows to a body length of 18 centimetres. Despite having many legs, millipedes are slow-moving creatures, so to protect themselves they coil their body into a spiral when threatened.

Giant rainforest bush cricket

A giant fire millipede in Madagascar

Largest beetle

The male rhinoceros beetle is instantly recognised by its long, curved horns. Some species are glossy and smooth, others are covered with hair. The goliath species grows to 18 centimetres. The horns are used for fighting with other males. They do not inflict damage, just warn the competition away.

The increasingly rare rhinoceros beetle

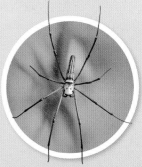

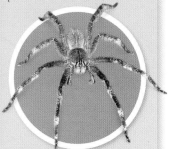

Reptiles and amphibians

In tropical rainforests there are **reptiles**, such as geckos, snakes, turtles and crocodiles; and **amphibians**, including frogs, toads and newts. The **herps** (the collective name for reptiles and amphibians) are equally at home high in the **canopy** or down in the **rivers** and among the fallen branches and leaf litter. From the large – a 227-kilogramme **anaconda** – to the tiny – a two-centimetre poison dart frog, the herps are **primitive** animals. Amphibians first gulped air **400 million** years ago, but in the last 30 years, 170 frog species have become **extinct**.

Facts

Reptiles	Amphibians
Examples Snakes, lizards, crocodiles, tortoises and turtles.	**Examples** Frogs, toads, newts and salamanders.
Method of breathing Lungs	**Method of breathing** Gills and lungs
Metamorphosis No. The young look like miniature adults when they are born.	**Metamorphosis** Yes. Young breathe water through gills until lungs develop.
Skin texture Dry and scaly. The scales are made of keratin.	**Skin texture** Smooth, moist and sometimes sticky, except for toads that have dry, warty skin.

Tiny snake

The Barbados threadsnake is believed to be the world's smallest snake. It measures only ten centimetres and feeds on insect larvae.

Carrying the kids

A female Suriname toad carries up to 100 eggs in a small depression on her back. The eggs hatch into fully-formed toads, skipping the larval (or tadpole) stage.

Herps are increasingly threatened by habitat loss, the pet trade and environmental change.

Did you know?

The yellow-spotted river turtle feeds on fruits, weeds, invertebrates and fish. It is one of the largest turtles in South America, reaching 45 centimetres and eight kilogrammes.

A green Madagascar gecko crawling on a tree

Camouflage skin

The oriental whip snake is a venomous snake most commonly found in Thailand's rainforests. Adults are a bright, almost fluorescent green, while juveniles may be yellow to pale brown. This elegant snake is perfectly camouflaged in the bushes and trees, so it can move around undetected.

Telescopic tongue

The panther chameleon's tongue is almost twice the length of its body (not including the tail). It is perfect for catching flies and spiders. It grows up to 50 centimetres. These chameleons can change the colour of their skin to blend in with its surroundings.

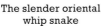
The slender oriental whip snake

A panther chameleon catching a cricket

Armoured skin

The dwarf caiman is the smallest living species of crocodile, growing to just 1.5 metres. It has the most protective bony plates on its skin of all caimans. When threatened, this caiman inflates its body and hisses. It is found in fast-moving waters, even waterfalls, of the Amazon and Orinoco rivers.

A dwarf caiman hunting in water

23

Plants of the rainforest

The humid conditions of the **rainforest** are perfect for plant growth. Plants have found ways to reach the upper, sunlit **layers** of the forest in order to **survive**. Some grow up the trunks of trees, while others establish themselves on **branches** and use their **roots** to extract nutrients from the moist air. Many rainforest plants rely on animals to **pollinate** and spread their seeds. In turn, animals depend on plants for food and **shelter**. Some plants and animals have special **relationships**, like the trap-jaw ants that **protect** the Costus plant while drinking its nectar.

More than two thirds of the world's plant species are found in the tropical rainforests.

A red-eyed tree frog looking out of a canna lily

Did you know?
The durian is thought to be one of Southeast Asia's most ancient trees. Animals eat its large, smelly fruit then excrete the seeds. This tree can live for 80 to 150 years.

Ancient plants
During an Ice Age, about 10,000 years ago, the polar ice caps spread but stopped short of the equator. This is why tropical rainforests and their plants survived to evolve.

Plant packed
A typical ten kilometre square area of tropical rainforest contains 1,500 kinds of flowering plants and 750 tree species!

The 'corpse flower' smells of rotting flesh

Rainforest flowers

To be pollinated or to have their seeds dispersed, plants use colour, smell and sweet nectar to attract insects and animals.

Heliconia

Its flowers come in a variety of colours. The flower is shaped so only a bird with a specialised beak can reach the nectar.

Big and smelly

The corpse or Rafflesia is the world's largest (up to one metre in diameter) and possibly smelliest flower. This rootless and leafless parasite grows inside a liana vine, until a bud breaks through the bark. It flowers every four years, is pollinated by flies and is often used in traditional medicines.

Air plants

Also called epiphytes, air plants often establish themselves on tree trunks. They extract nutrients from the air, not the soil. Their seeds or spores are often dropped into the canopy by birds and animals. They make their own energy, so do not feed on the host tree, but over time they can strangle it.

This fern, growing on a trunk, is an air plant

Bromeliad

There are 2,700 types of bromeliad, which includes the pineapple. The head of stiff leaves collects water, debris and animal life.

Carnivore plants

Nepenthes are tropical pitcher plants that get their nutrients from animal matter. Insects and small mammals are attracted to the colour, nectar and smell of these plants, but once inside cannot climb up its waxy walls. They drown in an acidic liquid that turns them into a nutritious, meaty soup.

Nepenthe are tropical carnivorous plants

Poinsettia

This festive plant has red leaves – they are not flowers. The leaves turn red only after a period of complete darkness.

25

People of the rainforest

Indigenous people have lived in the **rainforests** for thousands of years. **Indigenous** means that they originated in that place – it is their **home**. It is hard to say exactly how many people rely on the rainforest for food and shelter, as many **tribes** are still isolated. To these people, the **rainforest** is an enormous part of their **culture**, traditions and beliefs. Over centuries they have hunted, gathered and **grown** their food, always protecting the land that supported them. Rainforests contain **valuable** materials (like timber), which threaten **traditional** ways of life.

Facts and figures

Guarani
Population: 250,000
This large group of indigenous people live in several countries, including Paraguay, Argentina, Brazil, Bolivia and Uruguay.

Yanomami
Population: 32,000
Yanomami live in tribal territories along the borders of Venezuela and Brazil. They are threatened by mining, ranching and western diseases.

Kayapo
Population: 7,000
The Kayapo are indigenous people living in Brazil. Their first contact with the outside world occurred in 1960.

Matses
Population: 2,000
The Matses live in the Amazon rainforest of Peru and Brazil. The men and women rub poison from green tree frogs into their skin for courage.

A floating village on the banks of the Amazon river in Peru

Unique languages

The 400 tribes of the Amazon are diverse in culture, language and heritage. Each tribe has its own language. The Piraha language is now only spoken by 250 to 380 speakers.

Silent language

The Kuku-Yalanji tribe of north Queensland, Australia, have their own sign language that they use when hunting and silence is needed.

Did you know?

Thailand's Kayan Lahwi females, from age five, wear neck rings – a length of brass that is coiled around the neck. They only remove the coil so it can be replaced by a longer one.

In Brazil, 87 tribes disappeared between 1900 and 1950.

Skilled hunters

The Baka are hunter-gatherers located in the Central African rainforest. This pygmy tribe is famous for its hunting, music and dancing skills. The Baka use a variety of hunting techniques including poisoned arrows, bows, crossbows, spears and traps. They set dams and use nets to catch fish.

A Baka hunter of Central Africa

A Kamayurá fisherman

Fishing for food

The Kamayurá tribe live deep in the Amazon rainforest, around Lake Ipavu. They live in a national park, built to protect their way of life and keep out deadly infections. Fish has always been a staple of their diet – their culture forbids eating the meat of furred animals – but fish stocks are dwindling as the Amazon rainforest becomes hotter and drier and deforestation takes its toll.

Tribal warfare

The Dani live in west Papua, Indonesia. Old tiffs are settled by pretend and real battles using weapons made of rock, wood and bone. Though many wear modern clothes, some still retain their traditional attire.

The chief of a Dani tribe performs a fighting dance

Factfile

More native tribes

It is estimated there are 1,000 different rainforest cultures in existence. It is uncertain how many have disappeared altogether.

Huli – Papua New Guinea
This tribe hunt, gather and grow their food. They are known for being tall. The men paint themselves with colourful clay.

Batwa – Uganda, Africa
One of several pygmy tribes, these nomadic peoples had to leave their forest when it became a World Heritage Site.

Hmong – Southeast Asia
This tribe would grow their food, then move to a new site when crops were poor. Today, many still farm but they remain in one place.

Produce of the forests

Although only **rainforest** natives know its true bounty, rainforest produce can be found in things we use, **eat** or wear every day. Imagine if there was no coffee, rice, **chocolate** or sugar? The fabrics and **furniture** in your home could come from rainforest fibre and timber **sourced** from sustainable plantations. Even **trainer** soles are made with latex from rubber trees. Of more importance are the **medicines** that are derived from rainforest **plants**. These demands put extreme pressure on the rainforests. It is critical that we care for the rainforests that **provide** them.

Millions of people rely on bananas for a quarter of their daily calories.

Harvesting bananas from the Amazon rainforest

Did you know?

Rattan, often seen on furniture, comes from a palm native to tropical regions of Africa, Asia and Australia. Reserchers are experimenting to use rattan as artificial human bone.

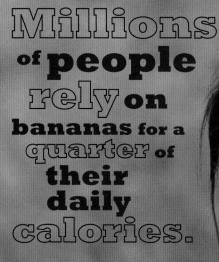

Rich with fruits

There are at least 3,000 different species of fruit growing in rainforests. Around 200 of these are now in use in the western world. Rainforest people eat over 2,000 fruit species.

Plant power

More than 2,000 tropical rainforest plants have been identified by scientists as having anti-cancer properties.

Ganoderma mushrooms

Natural medicines

The Ganoderma mushroom in Asian medicine aids health and a long life, and in western medicine it is being tested as a treatment for a wide range of diseases. It grows on woody trunks in warm, moist, mountainous Asian rainforests. Its commercial value grows as its medical uses increase.

Rubber tappers

Rubber tappers extract the milky sap (called latex) from rubber trees that grow wild in the Amazon rainforest. Tappers know that their livelihood relies on the trees, so they ensure the trees stay healthy. This has earned the tappers the name 'guardians of the rainforest'.

Palm oil

The reddish-coloured oil that comes from the fruit of the African oil palm has been used in cooking and cosmetics for many years, but now many baked goods and detergents contain palm oil. To meet the demand, areas of rainforest are being cleared and replanted with palms.

Latex being extracted from a rubber tree

Harvesting palm oil in Malaysia

Under threat

Many of the world's rainforests are under **threat**. Their trees are valuable felled (often **illegally**) as timber and the millions of hectares of land can be used for greater profit if **cleared** for intensive ranching and agriculture. **Deforestation** not only leads to the loss of many animal and plant **species**, but it also has a **dramatic** effect on the entire planet. Rainforests are unique ecosystems that provide an essential **environmental** service by continuously **recycling** carbon dioxide into the **oxygen** that our planet needs to survive.

Destroying rainforests in Borneo to make way for oil palm plantations

Facts and figures

Philippines
Between 1960 and 1990, 90 per cent of its rainforests were lost.

El Salvador
Bombing during the country's civil war (1984–1985) caused the loss of 85 per cent of its rainforests.

Madagascar
The island country of Madagascar, off Africa's east coast, has lost 95 per cent of its forests over the last 50 years.

Sumatra
The island of Sumatra has only 15 per cent of its rainforests left.

Central Africa
The Central African rainforests are the world's second largest, but only six per cent of them have been protected by law.

South America
The continent of South America has lost a total of 70 per cent of its rainforests.

Forest population

There were an estimated ten million native people living in the Amazon rainforest five centuries ago. Today, there are less than 200,000.

Going, going, gone?

There used to be 15 million square kilometres of tropical rainforest worldwide, but as a result of deforestation, only six million square kilometres currently remain intact.

Did you know?

You can help save rainforests by buying food that comes from sustainable sources. The Rainforest Alliance seal is a symbol of social, environmental and economic sustainability.

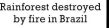
Rainforest destroyed by fire in Brazil

Burned down

There have always been rainforest fires, but a combination of deforestation, longer dry seasons and rising temperatures have meant more fires. One Amazon fire in 2007 burned an area equal to one million football pitches! When a rainforest is cleared, it releases gases, like carbon dioxide. These gases collect and prevent heat escaping, and so Earth's temperature increases.

Timber industry

In Columbia, 80 per cent of logging is illegal and done in a way that means regrowth is poor. But legal, sustainable logging allows long-term harvesting, replanting and conservation of the whole ecosystem.

Timber being taken from the rainforest in Borneo

The Amazon rainforest produces 20 per cent of the world's oxygen.

Amazon shrinking

Around 17 per cent of the Amazon rainforest has been lost in the last 50 years. Most of the cleared land has been used for rearing cattle.

Nature's thermostat

Rainforests help to regulate the temperatures and weather patterns of the whole world.

An endangered Sumatran orangutan

Habitat loss

The Indonesian rainforest habitat of the Sumatran orangutan is being cut down for timber or cleared for palm oil trees and farming. In addition, orangutans are hunted for the pet trade and only breed every six to seven years. Orangutans could be extinct in the wild in 25 years.

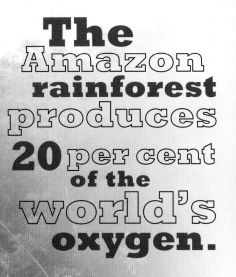

Glossary

Algae
A single or multi-cellular organism that has no roots, stems or leaves and is often found in water.

Amphibian
A cold-blooded, smooth-skinned animal, such as a frog, that lives on land but breeds in water.

Bacteria
Microscopic living organisms, usually one-celled, that can be found everywhere.

Bird
A warm-blooded animal, which has feathers, a beak, no teeth, wings and bears young in eggs.

Camouflage
Colours, patterns and shapes that make an animal difficult to see against its background.

Carnivore
An animal, or plant that kills and eats other animals.

Canopy layer
The leafy upper branches of rainforest trees. This layer is often densely covered with plants and tied together with vines.

Climate
The average weather conditions found in a particular region.

Continent
One of Earth's seven major areas of land.

Decomposer
An organism — usually a bacteria or fungus — that breaks down the cells of dead plants and animals into simpler substances.

Deforestation
The cutting down of forest trees for timber, or the clearing of land for farming or building.

Ecosystem
A community of plants or animals and the environment to which they are adapted.

Emergent layer
The uppermost layer of the rainforest, which consist of the tops of the tallest trees.

Environment
The external conditions or surroundings of a given organism.

Epiphytes
A plant that grows on another plant for support but does not extract nourishment from its host.

Equator
An imaginary line around Earth, which separates the Northern and Southern hemispheres.

Fermentation
A metabolic process that converts sugar to acids, gases or alcohol.

Foliage
The leaves of a plant or tree.

Forage
To search for and eat food.

Forest floor
The lowest layer of a rainforest, extending from the ground to about one metre high.

Humidity
A measurement of the amount of water vapour in the air.

Insects
A small animal that has six legs and generally one or two pairs of wings.

Invertebrates
A group of animals that do not have backbones.

Lichens
A complex organism made of a fungus joined with an algae. Lichens grow in leaf-like, crust-like, or branching forms.

Mammal
A warm-blooded animal that suckles it's young with milk and has a single bone in its bottom jaw.

Nutrients
A source of nourishment, such as food, that can be used by an organism to give it energy.

Organisms
Any form of animal or plant life. An organism consists of separate parts that work together to support its existence.

Photosynthesis
The process by which plants make food using sunlight.

Predator
An animal that lives mainly by killing and eating other animals.

Reptile
An animal with waterproof scaly skin, such as a lizard or snake, that typically lays eggs and lives on land.

Rodent
An animal with sharp incisors (front teeth) for gnawing, such as a mouse or squirrel.

Sediment
Material that is deposited by wind, water, or ice.

Scavenger
Scavengers are animals that feed on dead or injured animals.

Species
A group of similar living things that breed together in the wild.

Sunlight
The light and energy that comes from the Sun.

Toxins
A poison produced by certain animals, plants, or bacteria.

Tropics
The region of Earth round the equator, which has a warm, wet climate all year round.

Understory layer
The rainforest trees that form the layer below the canopy layer.

Index